THE MALADY LINGERS ON
And Other Great Groaners

I met a girl once, she was walking across the Pennines with a sack of wheat on her back. She said, 'Excuse me, do you know where there's an all-night windmill?'

I fell in love with her. I said, 'Darling, I could live in your eyes.' She took her teeth out of an apple and replied, 'You'd be at home, there's a sty in one of them'.

Oh, I know she was nothing to look at, she was so thin there was no point in her wearing a bra, I've seen bigger lumps in oatmeal. Her hair had been dyed so often she had technical dandruff.

But I can't forget her . . . I remember the rock garden where we got stoned together. The little things . . . the way she would stand in a chip pan and pretend she was a dipstick

Also in Arrow by Les Dawson

THE LES DAWSON JOKE BOOK

The Malady Lingers on
And Other Great Groaners

Les Dawson

Cartoons by Albert

ARROW BOOKS

Arrow Books Limited
17–21 Conway Street, London W1P 6JD

An imprint of the Hutchinson Publishing Group

London Melbourne Sydney Auckland
Johannesburg and agencies throughout
the world

First published 1982

Set in Times by Photobooks (Bristol) Ltd

Made and printed in Great Britain
by The Anchor Press Ltd
Tiptree, Essex

ISBN 0 09 929530 X

A WORD TO THE READER

'I wouldn't say that my wife is fat, but . . . she's
got a fat butt!' That play on words was first
uttered by one of my ancestors . . . Elric The
Peculiar, the only Viking ever to get mugged in
Gateshead. He was a round-shouldered little man
and his feet smelt. His wife was called Winifred
The Ready, and she sold unglazed chamber pots
to ferret trainers in the forests of Wolverhampton
– she was known locally as 'Winnie the Po'. They
begat a son who went mad in a box, and was
prone to applauding himself in a burial crypt,
hence the expression: 'Who crept in the crypt,
clapped and crept out again!'

Winifred had an affair with a Pict who, alas,
was chewed to death by a pole cat. Winifred never
got over it, and would sing this plaintive lament in
the wine shops . . . 'If I had a talking pict chewer
of you, hoo.' The Pict, however, had put a bun in
Winnie's oven so to speak, and as the snows
blanked out the green meadows, she gave birth to
a daughter – in an upright stance, because it was
too cold to lie down. It was a case of stand and
deliver. She christened the baby Friday because it
was so ugly she decided to call it a day.

As the girl grew to maturity, she changed her
name to Monday, because she hated being a
weekend. She was so awful to look at, a saying
arose in the wild Border area: 'If Rome wishes to

keep the barbarians at bay, don't let the Border see her'. The name stuck and was later abridged to Boadicea and she became Queen of the Iceni tribe and a celebrated lay.

Seth Dawson, a shepherd in Lambeth, coined a pun that will keep molars grinding for eons. It happened when a light 'plane was forced down in Potter's Bar, and out tottered a Turkish Bey, dizzy with the accident. Suddenly a trio of rams hove into view and the middle ram ate the Bey in one gulp. Seth was appalled. He sat on the pavement and sang: 'Middle ram you've had a dizzy Bey!' You see? T'was a play on words from a melody by Mr Bing Crosby entitled: 'Little man you've had a busy day!' Forget it.

I've done my best to keep up the tradition. On my wedding day, as I stood at the altar with the father-in-law's Luger firmly lodged in my upper spinal column, I wanly crowed a pun to show the world that I was not afraid. As my bride lurched down the aisle, looking rather like a reject from an audition for 'The Elephant Man', I chortled, 'Man cannot live by bride alone!' The vicar turned away and the best man beat me up behind the font.

At a recent chess congress, held in a cinema foyer, the manager was heard to yell: 'Get 'em all out . . . Get these chess nuts out of the foyer.'

When I toured Japanese working men's clubs last year (I had this yen to do it) those busy wee people obviously thought that I was an impressionist, because in one bird's nest soup factory canteen, they stood up after my act and shouted, 'Do Harry Karry.'

A pun helps to buck one up. When my laundry business was washed up, I didn't take a powder even though I had no money to *tide* me over. (The business was a *flash* in the pan.) *Surf*ice to say it was a case of *ariel* today and gone tomorrow, I *persil*lony vouch for that.

So do buy this book dear friend and with the hot cash advance I can seek treatment.

THE ART OF A PUN . . . OR HOW TO LOSE AN AUDIENCE FAST . . .

Puns, ah yes. My dear reader, you either love 'em or loathe 'em, there is no in between. Personally I love them; the challenge of a play on words fascinates me: it is stimulating, it gives one a broad range of our language, and gets rid of dull relatives very quickly.

I firmly believe that the art of punning needs a swift mind, high intelligence, and raw courage, especially if you are in a strange pub. For those of you who are still undaunted, enter now the world of the twisted wordsmith.

Let's begin by mangling a few song titles, starting with that old classic,

'I SAW YOU LAST NIGHT AND GOT THAT OLD FEELING'

So off you go and 'Pun my soul, I hope you have the stomach for it . . . As Ann Hathaway once said, as she tried to write a poem after leaving Shakespeare, 'These days I seem to go from bard to verse.'

Many years ago when Oldham was a wilderness of forest, tree fellers in the area were offered an incentive bonus to clear the densely wooded area in order to build a castle for a veteran Crusader, who had been knighted for kicking Saladin up the walls of Acre, thus giving his opponent two achers. Wimpey's got the job and Leyland Chariots went on a three day a week. The lads worked like stink and soon the forest shrank as the trees fell. The foreman kept a log book, which was oak with the workers who liked him because he was always spruce, and wasn't above putting silver in your palm, although the Lone Ranger wasn't too struck.

Tree felling is a prosperous business and soon they had branches everywhere which is only fir. All that was left was a mighty yew tree, and that was because the foreman, an ex-ballet dancer with a bad leg called Maurice – nobody knew what the other leg was called – promised the tree fellers that whoever did saw the yew down would be given an old tom cat for his supper. Remember, in those days meat was scarce and cats were considered a great delicacy, so one particular woodman kept on tackling the tree with only a slight paws in between. (Sorry, that *was* awful.)

His toil paid off. A month later he managed to saw down the mighty yew. The delighted foreman presented him with the tom cat and off he trotted to his humble dwelling to prepare the cat for his supper.

He said to his wife, 'Elsie, lass, bung that in't pot with some lentils and split peas.' His wife looked the cat over and said fearfully, 'Ere, you haven't pinched that moggie have you lad?' He shook his head. 'Nay, lass, I won it fair and square through sawing down a yew tree yesterday evening. That old cat is my reward . . . now, come on, cook it and we can have two legs purr person.'

His wife shoved the lot in the pot and as they watched it all come to the boil, the woodsman stood on a stool and sang in a rich baritone voice:

'I SAWED YEW LAST NIGHT AND GOT THAT OLD FELINE'

Last year my wife ran off with the fellow next door, and I must admit I still miss him. But I carried on looking after my two kids – it wasn't easy, the only way I could make ends meet was by putting them in the same nappy.

Yes, in those days I was really scraping the bottom, and getting behind in everything.

I managed to get a job, it wasn't much money but had plenty of time off . . . I was a Coronation Flag seller . . . I like a job with standards.

This next tooth grinding pun, is again quite an easy one, and might lull you into reading the rest of them, thus enabling me to buy the luxuries in life . . . bread and shoes.

I'm not saying things are bad, but I've been evicted from my flat so often for non-payment of rent, I've had the loose covers made to match the pavements.

Now, are you sitting comfortably? Well here's yet another garbled pun on the song:

'WAY DOWN UPON THE SWANEE RIVER'
(FAR FAR AWAY)

When I did my National Service, I used to sink water gourds in ice cold streams . . . Yes, I was a Cold Stream Gourds man.

Did you know that if you inject a carrot with influenza, it will attack onions? Are you aware that if a pigmy shaves the eyebrows off a middle-aged trout, he is then forbidden to wear a kilt?

One man knew all these things, a strange forbidding man who was a mystic swami from Huddersfield. I used to talk to him about such varied topics as the effect of double glazing on cows' udders and dental decay in the fang of a python. It was that sort of conversation . . . either one fang or an udder.

He was a very interesting man, tall, dark and aquiline of feature; dressed in an Inverness cape and Japanese gaiters, he always carried a leg of pork around with him . . . unusual, really, because it was still attached to the pig.

He was a keen football fan until Forfar Athletic let him down on a football pool. From then on revenge against that team was the theme of his life. He moved to Scotland, rented a room above a butcher's shop, and made his first diabolical move.

He cursed the team, sticking pins into effigies of the players. Soon the eleven players were suffering from backache, warts, acne and boils on the bum. He laid the curse to work only when Forfar Athletic played at home – their away matches didn't matter – and soon of course the supporters lost interest and took up needlework. Everyone was frantic, the swami was Public Enemy No. 1, but no way could be found of getting at him – until one day the butcher downstairs, having just served the swami with his favourite meat, lamb's liver, saw the swami grow rigid and his eyes became glazed. For an hour he stood rooted to the spot, unable to move. The butcher said 'I can't understand it . . . I weighed his liver on the scales and he went like that!' His assistant looked at the scales and said, 'The scales are faulty, you've charged him too much, and if you do that in Huddersfield it can cause a coma.' Now the butcher knew how to combat the mystic swami and the following week when the swami came in for his liver, the butcher said, 'Here's our chance, the team's away so let's cheat the swami.' His assistant said 'How?' and the butcher sang:

'WEIGH DOWN UPON THE SWAMI'S LIVER
FORFAR'S AWAY'

I met a girl once, she was walking across the Pennines with a sack of wheat on her back. She said, 'Excuse me, do you know where there's an all-night windmill?'

I fell in love with her. I said, 'Darling I could live in your eyes.' She took her teeth out of an apple and replied, 'You'd be at home, there's a sty in one of them.'

Oh, I know she was nothing to look at. She was so thin there was no point in her wearing a bra, I've seen bigger lumps in oatmeal. Her hair had been dyed so often she had technical dandruff.

But I can't forget her . . . I remember the rock garden where we got stoned together. The little things . . . the way she would stand in a chip pan and pretend she was a dipstick . . .

Still, there are other fish in the sea, and I'm now married to a pike . . . Her father is a doctor, a member of the Royal College of Sturgeons. His brother sings, he's a bass. He's a shrimp but hard as snails . . . mussels everywhere. Dances well, does the conger.

I had fun with this following play on words, the only one who did, it's a gobbet of gaiety on the song:

'WHEN THE MIDNIGHT CHOO CHOO LEAVES FOR ALABAM'

> I don't like trains, the goods waggons 'freighten' me, besides I get a tender behind. Diesel the things that scare me.

India is a sub-continent that holds so many secrets. From the purple hills of the Punjab to the steaming delta of the Ganges, the vast country grips you like a bad curry in Bradford. I spent two years in India, I was a janitor in a karate clinic, the wages were lousy but there were plenty of back handers. With only a soiled saffron coloured robe to cover me, carrying my begging bowl, I roamed the hot land in search of Truth . . . and I found it in the silent monastery of Kala, a holy place often visited by Mather, the great explorer, who constructed a water tap for the monks to douse themselves with, hence the words of the old song: 'On Mather Kala's Douse Tap.'

I met an old, wise man who had spent a hundred years just sitting on a stone slab. I asked him what he had found in all his years of contemplation. He spoke in a low voice that sounded like a thousand winds sighing on the rocks below. He waved his hands that were simply withered leaves of aged tissue and he said to me, 'Sitting here on this gnarled boulder has given me wisdom, my son, tolerance, inner understanding and piles.' I never forgot the old man and went on to a new task: circumsizing elephants. Not much of a salary, but the tips were enormous.

It was in Bombay that I met Mr Baum, a chemist from Crewe, who was trying to find a cure for his son's neck defect. Mr Baum's son, Alan, had suffered for years and every type of treatment had been attempted but to no avail. But from the lips of a fakir, hope at last flickered. The fakir told Baum: 'Take the leaves from the sacred tanna tree, have them chewed into a pellet by a chow

17

dog that belongs to an insane knight of the British realm, and all will be well with Alan Baum.' They discovered a cracked baron living in Ormskirk; he had a chow bitch and they had it brought to India to chew the leaves of the tanna tree. The animal did so, the mess was slapped on Alan Baum's neck and lo! the lad was cured, and everybody sang:

'WHEN THE MAD KNIGHT'S CHOW CHEWS LEAVES FOR ALAN BAUM'

The Great Wall of China was built with the sweat of coolie labour only; it survives to this day. The Pyramids of Egypt were erected by slaves, using only a primitive knowledge; they shadow the desert still. Last week, a team of highly trained construction workers built me a brick garage using modern technology; yesterday it fell down.

Everybody's lazy these days, the other morning I had to shout to the wife twice to come upstairs and dress me.

We can sure learn a lot from history if we'd only take the trouble to do so, and the pun you are about to revel in has a historical theme . . . Rome no less. When Caesar was asked when he first arrived on these shores if he thought the British fogs were the worst in the world, he craned his neck, rubbed his sore eyes and said: 'I agree . . . I craned, eyes sore, I concur.'

I'll *have* to have treatment . . . especially after this song title:

'I'M GETTING SENTIMENTAL OVER YOU'
(WHEN SHADOWS FALL, OVER SLEEPY
GARDEN WALLS)

There used to be a German sentry outside the Doge's Palace in Venice and he bit people . . . Hence the saying: 'The Herr of the Doge that bit me.'

I got up early last Tuesday morning which was very handy, because I had the rest of the day to myself. The wife was still asleep like a baby . . . with her big toe in her mouth. As per the norm she had mud on her face and her hair was in curlers. I never get used to it, it's like being in bed with a sort of transistorized bog . . . I don't know why she really bothers, I'm not saying the wife's ugly but every time she puts make up on the lipstick backs into the tube.

I went downstairs to put the kettle on, but it didn't fit, my arm got caught up the spout twice. Our donkey was sprawled on the rug, it's not a pet, we just have it for kicks. We used to have a small constrictor as a pet but it turned out to be a boa.

Just then there was a tap on the door and I thought 'I must have a word with that plumber'. I opened the paint-peeled portal and the wife's mother was stood there in the pouring rain. I said, 'Don't stand there getting wet . . . go home.'

Suddenly the telephone rang and a historian friend of mine on the other end of the line told me a little known fact about the Roman Empire. It was so stunning, I mixed myself a Little David cocktail. They're so strong if you have more than two, you have to 'Goliath' down.

The information was this: Slaves on the Nile used to shear the barnacles and fungus from the bottoms of the Arab dhows and sometimes the dhows would fall over and crush the poor devils. The slaves were guarded by mercenaries from Gaul, and the heat of the Middle East made them sleepy. The acid from the barnacles underneath the dhows irritated the skin quite a lot, and the only soothing balm available was highly perfumed lentils. One day an Arab dhow fell on top of the Gauls acting as wardens over the slaves. The wretched men moaned as the acid burned through their leather trousers, and a foreman stood on a hill and sang this timeless lament:

'WHEN SHEARED DHOWS FALL, OVER
SLEEPY WARDEN GAULS. . .
I'M GETTING SCENTED LENTILS OVER YOU'

I like trees, that's why I keep myself clean and spruce. Every time I plant another tree my wife says, 'I'm sycamore trees.' My garden is so small, the worms are round-shouldered.

My next door neighbour's wife is a most peculiar woman. Last week she stood in a fish pond pouring grass seed over her head. I said, 'What are you doing that for?' She whispered, 'I want to be a lawn.' My soil is rotten, if a vegetable does happen to grow it's certainly a turnip for the book, it's a good thing gardening isn't my job, I would never earn a celery . . . It's sure got me beet. If anyone could give me a tip or two, I'd be very peased, and I've bean around a long time, so lettuce hope things improve quite shallot.

It was the struggle with the earth that prompted this most extraordinary play on words. The song from which the words are culled is:

'MAMMA'S LITTLE BABY LOVES SHORTENIN' BREAD'

Use your loaf with this one, and it will roll off your tongue and you'll feel butter for it. And don't forget, I knead the dough.

Not many people know this fact, but for some years I was a 'Private Eye', well-respected with two bright pupils. It wasn't an easy job; let's face it, not every Tom and Harry can be a Dick. During my years as an investigator, I had been shot at, poisoned and stabbed . . . then, mercifully the wife went back to her mother.

My most baffling case concerned a midget

gents' barber who worked for a lapsed Mormon. The tiny hairdresser was so small his chin had a rash from his bootlaces, and when he pulled his underpants up he blindfolded himself. This dwarf had a burning hatred of anybody who was taller than he was. In particular, he loathed Reginald Maudling the well-known politician. One day he kidnapped the statesman, strapped him down on a table in a wood shed, took the poor man's shoes off and started to whittle him away with a joiner's plane. I rushed to the scene and tried to talk the frenzied midget out of committing the abominable act.

The dwarf merely glared at me and carried on shaving layers of Maudling's feet with evident relish. I backed out of the shed and, looking around me at the horrified crowd, I sang plaintively:

'MORMON'S LITTLE BARBER LOVES
SHORTENIN' MAUDLING, MORMON'S LITTLE
BARBER LOVES SHORTENIN' REG'

24

I once painted a girl in the nude – well not entirely, I kept my socks on so I had somewhere to put my brushes.

I tried my hand at painting for many years and produced many masterpieces, such as:

'The Frowning Cavalier'
'Whistler's Father'
'Elsie Lisa'

I can't imagine where I went wrong.

Below, I have contrived to twist out of all proportion a well known song:

'MY EYES HAVE SEEN THE GLORY OF THE COMING OF THE LORD' (AS WE GO MARCHING ALONG)

I keep fit by having a pinta milk a day. I used to bath in milk, someone said: 'Pasturised?' I said 'No just up to my knees.' It's enough to make your stomach churn.

I love all art, in particular the great masters who live forever through their work: Rembrandt, Monet, Degas, Leonardo da Vinci, whose 'Mona Lisa' enthralls me. I took the wife to Paris to see that marvellous painting, I said to her, 'You are about to see the Mona Lisa.' She replied: 'I didn't know the Isle of Man boats came this far.' Typical retort. I'm not saying the wife is ignorant, but she thought camiknickers were people who stole soap. She honestly thought that rabies was something you got if you bit a Jewish vicar. A

25

chap called at the house once, he said to the wife, 'I'm collecting for Lord Derby's trust fund.' The wife said, 'I didn't even know he was ruptured.' She gets worse, if brains were elastic, she wouldn't have enough for a frog's jock strap.

I heard that a painting, an original I might add, by Lowry, was to be seen in house near my digs in Leeds. I like Leeds, it's a sort of thinking man's Bradford without curry. I went to the place and was shown around the old dwelling by a butler who was German by birth. I said to him, 'Born in Germany hey? Which part?' He said, 'All of me.' He was a nice sort of chap with a jackboot rash, and he explained to me that the Lowry was so valuable it was kept in a cupboard by the owner who, it transpired, was a retired Scottish Laird from Perthshire.

He took me all over the house. It was crammed with treasures: tapestries, gold ornaments from the East and, most impressive of all, a door that belonged to William the Conqueror . . . You could see his initials on it: 'W.C.'

The butler went into the kitchen and brought out two ice creams, and off we went again licking our ices. Finally, we came to the cupboard where the Laird kept the Lowry painting and with rising excitement I watched the butler open the cupboard door. As he did so his ice cream dropped onto the painting and as he tried to wipe it off, it stained the canvas. The butler was frantic and he wailed to me:

'MEIN ICE HAS STAINED THE LOWRY IN THE CUPBOARD OF THE LAIRD AS WE GO MUNCHING A CONE'

How, you may well ask, can anyone possibly make a mess out of such a simple pop tune as:

'I NEVER FELT MORE LIKE SINGING THE BLUES (I NEVER THOUGHT THAT I'D EVER LOSE YOUR LOVE)'

I did, and now await deportation.

For years I attended a school that specialized in the teaching of correct English Grammar. When I left, the headmaster said: 'Dawson I wish you all the best in the field of journalism.' I replied: 'Thank you sir, you was very good to me . . .'

After you've read this one, don't ask for any money back, to coin a phrase, just stay in a pence-if mood. I'm being franc now so I deserve full marks. Otherwise I'll be in the dollardrums.

Everyone has a family tree; the Dawsons have one, it's a weeping willow. My family can trace its roots back to Elric The Peculiar, the first Viking to be mugged in Gateshead.

He married Grizelda, the daughter of a blacksmith. She used to help her father at work: when the horse was ready for shoeing, she'd hand him the horse.

She was a big lass with many things that men admire . . . muscles, hair and duelling scars. She was so fat, when she bent down in Newcastle, they had an eclipse in Bournemouth. They had a son who was so ugly they had to put shutters on his pram. Despite his looks however, he did well for himself. He married a shortsighted woman who later went bald in a box, she had a bob or two, as a child she used to get boys at school in a corner and say, 'Give me a penny or a kiss.' By the time she was fifteen she owned a Rolls Bentley.

So you can see I'm fond of history and all that and the Tudor Period is the one I like most. Not many scholars are aware for instance that Sir Thomas More used to work in a laundry – yes, startling isn't it? In fact More was beheaded not for treason, but for an entirely different reason.

Henry sent his wife's blouse to More's laundry and he wanted it cleaned and ironed. Alas, Thomas had been at the mead, and he was slightly Brahms and Lizt . . . he singed the blouse. Henry was very angry when he heard the news and he stormed out of his bath, and flung his wife's best loofah into the moat and lost it. Queen Anne went up the wall and demanded More's death, and Henry, for the sake of peace and quiet, agreed. Thomas More was brought into the courtyard, made to kneel and was then tarred and feathered first before being beheaded. Henry turned to his wife and sang softly:

'I FEATHERED KNELT MORE FOR SINGEING
   THE BLOUSE,
I NEVER THOUGHT THAT I'D EVER LOSE
   YOUR LOOFAH.
THAT'S WHY I'M SINGING THE BLUES'

I had a lot of fun with this song title – plus half a bottle of gin. My grandfather died through drink, he fell in a vat of whiskey, and it took him five hours to drown, mind you he got out of the vat three times to go to the Gents'.

He was cremated, and we'll never know just how much of the stuff he swallowed, but it took three months to put the fire out. The song title in question is:

'FALLING IN LOVE AGAIN, WHAT AM I TO DO? WHAT AM I TO DO? I CAN'T HELP IT'

My wife's lips are so big when I kiss her it's like being attacked by an innertube. No wonder she's often tyred. Wheel, that's my problem, and sometimes I go spare. Aren't tyres dear? It's rubbery with violence. One has to be careful where one treads.

I did my stint in the army thanks to National Service, and I was a good little soldier, in fact I was asked if I would take a commission. I said no, I much preferred a straight salary. I had only been in the service for six months when I was court-martialled for sleeping in in the mornings; the commanding officer said, 'Dawson, don't you hear the bugle in the morning?' I replied with spirit, 'No sir, they always play it whilst I am asleep.' Mind you, I come from a military family – you've heard of the Thin Red Line? Well, we were the Fat Yellow Blob. My Great Great Grandfather Tobias Dawson fought with Wellington . . . they couldn't trust him with a gun, he eventually got the boot and that just goes to shoe you. Emmerdale Dawson was with General Custer at the Little Big Horn, when the famous Indian fighter said: 'I will wear my red britches so that the red-skins won't see the blood . . . What will you wear Dawson?' Emmerdale replied: 'Khaki'.

During the First World War, Quentin Dawson was on the Somme when the first shot was fired; he was under a bed in Crewe when the second one went off. However, I was posted to Germany and it was in Munich that I met a beautiful woman who looked like Marlene Dietrich. She was a forelady in charge of a bakery but alas, business was bad because something was wrong with the quality of her bread, no matter what she did she failed with her loaves. The problem was mice living in the stream that supplied the water for the bread, got into the dough mix and ruined it. A health inspector gave her some advice; he told her to put talcum powder inside the pit where she put the dough, and that would get rid of the rodents. The trouble was she couldn't reach into the pit to place the talcum in it, and she grew very unhappy and started to drink heavily. The last time I saw her, she was sat in a Berlin night club and she was singing sadly:

'FAILING IN LOAVES AGAIN, WATER MICE TO DOUGH, WATER MICE TO DOUGH, I CAN'T TALC PIT'

I hesitated with this one, after all, it is a hymn, and the last thing I want is to upset religious people. I'm very fond of our local vicar and when he came to see us the other day, it was to inform us that he was leaving the parish. My wife, bless her, said to him, 'Everybody will be sorry to see you go vicar, because nobody knew what sin was until you came.'

For better or for worse here is my version of

'OH GOD OUR HELP IN AGES PAST'

Sermon of these days, I'll go to church again, after all I haven't altared. My sister went out with a clergyman but he nearly rector. Nun of these things apply really, so I'll Pope out for a bit.

I went to see our doctor last week, I stood in his surgery coughing and sneezing and he said: 'Flu?' I said, 'No, I came on the bus'. He's not a very good doctor, in fact he's so old-fashioned when he lances a boil he does it on horseback. He doesn't believe in pain killers . . . he makes you bite on a bullet . . . Actually he's retiring soon, he's running out of leeches.

'How do I stand?' I asked him. He said, 'It's a bloody mystery to me.'

He examined me and pointed to a bottle on a high shelf. 'Do me a sample in that bottle,' he said. I replied, 'What, from down here.'

As I was leaving I said to him, 'Can you help me out then?' He said, 'Certainly, which way did you come in?' Actually he gave me some medicine to take after a hot bath, but could I swallow it? It took me all my time drinking the bath water.

I was off work after that, and took to going to the local library. On one visit I came across a book which gave a new insight on the Bible. Did you know dear reader, that at one period of time in the Holy Land, money was unknown? Well it's true, they used pea pods as currency in Bethlehem.

Even in those days, crime was a problem and one arch criminal, by the name Aja, had a son who couldn't keep his hands off the pea pods, he was in every sense a pest. The people made hoops of strong basket weave; these were used to throw over runaway crooks to halt their flight, and very effective they were.

One pay day, Aja's son held the local bank up, took all the pea pods they had, and managed to escape the fury of the citizens. There was an uproar over the robbery and the Jewish priests formed a posse – there were a lot of them, after all they breed like Rabbis.

'Attention citizens,' one dignified Rabbi shouted. 'Aja's son has stolen all our gelt, our pea pods, but we've got our hoops and we'll have him, so don't worry.' Upon hearing this, all the people stood and sang the old hymn:

'OH PODS OUR GELT IN WAGES SNATCH,
    OUR HOOPS FOR AJA'S PEST'

I have always been interested in politics, my father was a socialist – well he must have been, because my mother was never out of the Labour Ward. My wife's family always vote Labour . . . they have to, they can't spell Conservative. I myself once stood as an Independent candidate, I only got three votes and that was after a recount. At the last General Election I said to the wife, 'Come my little turtle dove, let us go and exercise our franchise.' She said, 'No, I've only just made the beds.'

You are now about to see for yourselves how easy it is to mangle the old Al Jolson song:

'ROCKABYE YOUR BABY WITH A DIXIE
MELODY'

I like rock gardens, I often get stoned in them. It's not easy to do, one has to be boulder than the others, especially in Peebles. That's the sort of remark that gets slated, mind you in Russia, they'd pay you in rubbles.

One of the world's great classical cookery dishes is the Goole Expanding Rissole. It's about four inches long and when crushed under a duck's armpit, it spits out braised lentils and whistles. You then strain it through a damp biscuit and warm it up in a pan of fresh fog. Some people smack it with a trowel, and pull it up the A1 towards Musselboro and leave it sweating in an overcoat until the wind comes up.

The wheat for this delicious titbit is only found in a small village near Gateshead, a village so old the thatched cottages are rinsed every day with Grecian 2000.

When I first went there, I was stunned at the sheer antiquity of the place, and the stories that sprang from its history. For instance, President Nixon of the United States once stayed in the village when he was a Boy Scout. During a storm he sheltered under an elm, and was saved from a bolt of lightning. He was so thankful he decided to save the elm, which had been badly damaged during the storm, and he had it pickled in his memory. The tree stood for many years, superbly mellowed.

Some years later, Amos Jugg, a local character, began to suffer from fits, and his mother in despair chained him to the mellowed elm to restrain him. But lo! Amos got better, and from that time on the tree was regarded as having magical powers; indeed, it cured ringworm, gout, palsy, boils; the list was endless. One day, a Jewish window cleaner arrived in the village with his wife, Becky, and only child, a boy called Abie. It seemed that the lad suffered from shingles and insomnia and he was getting worse. The only time the boy nodded off was when his mother rocked him in her arms for an hour.

Abie's father was impatient to get going and he said to his wife, 'Golda, start rocking our son to sleep, then bind him to the tree quickly.' His wife, who was hard of hearing, said, 'I can't hear you too well.' So the Jewish window cleaner sang:

'ROCK AND BIND YOUR ABIE TO A NIXON
MELLOWED TREE'

I used to work on a farm as a pilot – I used to pile it here and pile it there . . . I fell in love with the farmer's daughter called Daisy, because she grew wild in the woods. She was a fine lass, a red head – no hair, just a red head. I tried my hand at milking just to impress her . . . the cow sat through it all mooing lovingly. I said to Daisy, 'This cow's enjoying it.' She said: 'I'm not surprised, you've got hold of the bull.' I had to leave the farm after that because the bull wanted to get engaged.

Let's take a musical, 'Porgy and Bess', and this tune:

'IT AIN'T NECESSARILY SO, NO IT AIN'T
    NECESSARILY SO,
THE THINGS THAT YOU'RE LIABLE TO READ
    IN THE BIBLE,
IT AIN'T NECESSARILY SO'.

And boy can you have a ball with it . . .

I like animals, in particular the Aardvark, after all 'aardvark never killed anybody. That is a Gnu joke although let's ape they get better.

In the Deep South, way past the Mason Dixon line, stood a house that was so big that when it was four o'clock in the kitchen it was half past seven in the lavatory, so large that the mice wore St Christopher medals, and there was a compass on the Hoover. The vast place belonged to a certain Miss Nestor the boss of a highly successful plantation; her favourite pastime was to make her slaves throw a German Mauser pistol into a pile of discarded coffee dregs, and then she'd sing in a rich baritone voice, 'Mauser's in de cold cold grounds'.

Miss Nestor had a prize pig, a huge old sow that often appeared in concerts. It had a fine tenor voice, and was often asked to sty on for an encore. The pig became so famous it was put under contract to an agent, and was given a monthly salary. Working for Miss Nestor was a shifty eyed man who was determined to steal the pig from his employer, and breed it with his friend's bull. This friend was an Indian from Bombay, and if the mating succeeded, they would have produced an animal that provided beef and bacon at the same time, thus making a fortune for them. The Indian was only a boy and didn't understand the villainy of the plot.

One night the man who worked for Miss Nestor stole the pig, put a label on it and let it run with some other pigs to divert suspicion.

Alas when it came time to do the actual mating he put the label on the wrong pig, and the whole thing was a mess. His wife, a strapping coloured lady, pointed out the error and sang:

'IT AIN'T NESTOR'S SALARY SOW . . . NO IT
    AIN'T NESTOR'S SALARY SOW . . .
THE THING THAT YOU LABELLED TO BREED
    INDIA BOY'S BULL,
IT AIN'T NESTOR'S SALARY SOW'

A LITERARY INTERLUDE

Let us pause awhile, dear, dear reader, and allow the depression caused by purchasing this tome of tripe to subside. Okay, you must be saying by now, anyone can mangle song titles, but what about twisting old Will Shakespeare a bit? 'Now is the winter of our discontent made glorious summer by this son of York'. Impossible to shred that? Wrong. Thanks to a sex-fevered imagination and a firkin of ale, I have done so, not wisely but too well.

Also there are a few quotes, sayings, book titles: all knotted in grotesque shapes, and it's up to you, friend, to sort 'em out. Hopefully when you do, I'll be in Cannes with a free-thinking nymphomaniac having naughties in a rented villa.

Richard the Third was a nice chap, even-tempered although from time to time he was known to get the hump. He had a nose for a bargain and always followed his hunch. He was very fond of the sea and for some little while, he lived in a council flat in Blackpool. It was in that most regal of resorts that he founded a flourishing business: a disco in a big tent, looked after by his best mate Noel, who was also a famous wine vintner from the vineyards at Crewe. Noel's chief claim to fame was his glorious mead which he brewed in the city of

York, in a sauna bath complex. The secret of the mead was in the simmering of the liquid, and it was very popular. Richard was very proud of his friend Noel, and would often make this stirring speech about him:

'NOEL IS THE VINTNER OF OUR DISCO TENT,
MEAD GLORIOUS SIMMER BY THIS SAUNA
YORK'

Some years ago, a nice chap called George Hamlet and his son met a strange looking woman known to all and sundry as 'Withered Tess' on account of the fact that she had been born with very thin limbs. She was a good person and the only one in the area who would cheerfully listen to George Hamlet's brother Reg, play his folk tunes, which frankly were awful – so much so that to stop the neighbours from lodging complaints, Reg would sit down a disused coal mine and try to iron out the errors in his folk tunes. (Mostly caused by use of slang expressions!)

As time went on, Withered Tess became a saint to the locals, and the parish priest publicly blessed her for her good works, while she, fine lady that she was, sat down the mine listening to Reggie all day.

Hamlet's eldest lad Otto was a farmer who had problems with a veritable sea of truffles encroaching into his pastures and upsetting his cows, and it cost money to keep the darned truffles at bay. It was a friend of his called Aron who kept giving him grants to pay for stuff to get rid of the truffles. Hamlet and his son were to find why some tower blocks built as luxury flats on the beach, were slipping into the sea after high tide, also causing drainage problems on a worrying scale.

(Are you still with it all? I'm not and I'm writing the damn stuff.)

So dawned the day when George Hamlet and his lad Alf set forth to Torbay. His son had never been away from home before and asked his dad if all the people they knew would be alright whilst they were away. George patted his boy on the

head and said in a confident voice: 'Fear not
Alfred they're okay, now we sally forth to inspect
Torbay, mainly in the centre of the town and
possibly in the north of the place . . . Come on son
here's old Rube Jackson to take us in his car . . .
Off we go my son . . . or as Shakespeare would
have said:

TORBAY OR NORTH TORBAY: THAT IS THE
    QUEST, SON;
WITHERED TESS NOW BLESSED IN THE MINE
    TO SAVOUR
THE SLANG AND ERRORS OF OUR REGGIE'S
    FOLKTUNES,
OTTO TAKES ARON'S GRANT, A SEA OF
    TRUFFLES
AND BY OPPOSING END THEM. TODAY
    TOWER'S SLIP
. . . POOR CHANCE TO DRAIN, AYE, THERE'S
    TH'OWD RUBE . . .

*'The quality of mercy is not strained,
It droppeth as the gentle rain from Heaven,
Upon the place beneath'*

Shakespeare never wrote that phrase, which appears in 'The Merchant Of Venice'. That speech came from Liverpool. Many years ago on the banks of the river Mersey, there was a tree that had been planted by an Australian vet whose pet Koala bear used to climb up a lot. The Australian's name was Ned and he adored his Koala bear's tree. A lot of people disliked the tree and often tried to get the council to shift it, but to no avail. Although Ned was Jewish, his best friend was a Gentile called Ryan, and he lived in Stratford-upon-Avon. The tree always made Ryan feel sorry for himself – why, nobody knew, but he was an ardent fisherman who sold plaice for a living.

One day, a crowd gathered on the heath to protest against the tree, and nothing would shift them. One councillor from Bootle had the idea to protect the tree by disguising it as a bush but when Ryan arrived, looking very fed up because his catch of plaice was rotten, a further plan became clear to the councillor.

'Ryan!' he said, 'slit open your fish and the wind will carry the stench to the crowd and when they start holding their noses, we can set fire to the grass on the heath and disperse the mob!'

The tree was hidden by branches to look like a bush, and just then Ned came along and cried aloud: 'Bloody hell! Someone's pinched my Koala tree!' The councillor put his arm around

Ned's shoulder and said, 'Not everybody hates the tree Neddy, your mate Ryan loves it even though it makes him sad, and he's here with your tree which is still here ... But we must act quickly! And the councillor stood and cried aloud:

'THE KOALA TREE OF MERSEY, IS NOT
    STRAYED NED.
IF DRAW PATHOS AS THE GENTILE RYAN'S
    FROM AVON
OPEN THE PLAICE! BURN HEATH!'

In a remote area of Mexico (in winter it gets very chilli there and the favourite song is: 'Sombrero-ver the Rainbow') lived a powerful landowner named Count Ray. He became respected when he freed all the slaves who worked as ranch hands for him. The freed hands stayed in the area and formed a sort of community farm, helped by another famous family called the Ramons. (One of the Ramon brothers climbed a mountain and crowned the summit with a flag every year on a Wednesday; he was the eldest son and his christian name was Shelby. Even today, strolling minstrels can be heard singing once a year: 'Shelby Ramon crowns the mountain Wednesday comes!')

Meanwhile, back in Mexico with the freed ranch hands, the Ramons and Count Ray and his men, peace reigned until a priest took over the parish. The priest was not a nice person and he hated children so much he confiscated their school see-saw and refused to let anybody borrow it. Nobody dared to defy the priest until the school master decided to confront the holy man, and so one night, he called a meeting of all the freed hands, Ramons and Count Ray's men who had children at his school, and he outlined his plan: to march with the children to the church and borrow the see-saw. The school master stood in front of the parents and declaimed:

'FREED HANDS, RAMONS AND COUNT RAY'S MEN . . . LEND ME YOUR HEIRS, I COME TO BORROW SEE-SAW, NAUGHTY PRIEST HIM'

*'O Romeo, Romeo. Wherefore art thou Romeo?
Deny thy father and refuse thy name'*

Immortal lines indeed from 'Romeo and Juliet',
but that speech was nicked by Old Will. You see,
many years ago in Venice, the finest canal
oarsman was Mio Giovanni, and he was also a
football referee.

It was the custom in Italian football to hold a
fancy dress ball after a match, and when they
played Wales in the European Cup, the captain
of Wales, one Nye Bevan, dressed up as a giant
bird, feathers, beak, the lot. Mio was away taking
a party of Americans up the canals on the night of
the ball, when a fight broke out between the
Welsh team and some Italian supporters. During
the fracas, Nye Bevan's leg feathers were ripped
apart and needed darning together.

Someone shouted that Mio was needed to
restore order, and as the referee had a strong
personality it was felt he was the man to put an
end to the brawl. However, as many people were
trying to gatecrash the party, they suggested that
Mio should don four of his boatman's hats so that
he would be recognized. Off went the man to find
Mio and eventually he spotted him rowing along
the Grand Canal. 'Put four hats on and row home
Mio' the man shouted. 'And when you get here use
your name to stop the fight.' Mio cupped his ear
and yelled back: 'What did you say?' The reply
became a must for all lovers of good literature:

'O ROW HOME MIO! ROW HOME MIO . . .
WEAR FOUR HATS THOUGH ROWIN' HOME
    MIO.
DARN NYE'S THIGH FEATHER AND REF. USE
    THY NAME'

Julius Caesar arrived in the British Isles and the first thing he spotted was a very old Iceni tribesman's embossed chamber pot, obviously jerry built so he gave his mate a tinkle in China . . . Caesar was not an emotional man, in fact he could be most po-faced, and yet he couldn't take his eyes off the chamber pot which frankly, was an eyesore, and used at the time for storing horse chestnuts. Old Julius was intrigued by the use that the ancient Britons put to horse chestnuts . . . a sort of sport called 'Conkers'. He fell for the game hook, line and sinker. Soon he became a past master at conkers and coveted the chamber pot as a means of storing his rich hoard of prize-winning chestnuts. One Bank Holiday Monday, he laid claim to the chamber pot and let his gladiators go to Ascot for the day.

Caesar was proud and he summoned his troops before him and as he held the chamber pot high in the air, he boomed loudly:

'I CLAIM EYESORE I CONKERED'

When I was a boy, my family was so poor, my dad used to mug tramps. The trouble was my father was very superstitious and he wouldn't work if there was a Friday in the week. Don't get me wrong, I'm not saying he was lazy, but he once fell asleep running for a bus. I said to him once: 'Daddy, why don't you get out of bed and have a walk round outside?' He said, 'Son, Opportunity only knocks once and I want to be in when it calls.'

He was a fine looking man: didn't smoke, didn't drink and made all his own frocks. He spent years on the dole and in ten years he was only offered one job . . . apart from that, they'd shown him nothing but kindness.

We lived in a house that was so small, when the town hall threatened us with eviction, they flushed us out with ferrets. Our house was in Miracle Road . . . so called because it was a miracle the houses were still standing. When they came to demolish our house to make way for a swamp, the corporation had to repair it first so it was safe to pull down . . . Still we were happy on the whole (that's what the house was – a hole).

One day we went to church for a wedding and the priest looked at us all after the ceremony and thundered: 'Look at you all, sinners, backsliders, the stench of corruption assails me . . . But let me warn you now . . . On the day of judgement most terrible there will be a wailing and a gnashing of teeth.' The priest leaned forward and hissed: 'Teeth will be provided.' My dad started to run towards the priest and before we could stop him, he had thrown Domestos all over his cassock. He was arrested and was charged with . . .

A BLEACH OF THE PRIEST

I have many happy memories of Scotland, and in particular, Forfar. I took a photograph of the wife in a fawn kilt, and everybody swore it was a snap of Ben Nevis . . . I'm not saying the lass is fat, but they used her knickers as a model for high rise flats. Anyway, whilst in Scotland, I heard a story that proves Charles Dickens was a plagiarist.

In his book, *A Tale of Two Cities*, Sydney Carton intones the lines: 'Tis a far, far better thing that I do than I have ever done before.'

In actual fact, he pinched that statement from a wee man in Forfar who had the sole concession for string, and because it was in short supply, he used the stuff as we would use money. He would barter it for other goods.

During a religious upheaval, all Druids were hunted down and had their cassocks shortened, which can be a problem if you haven't got a hem on the bottom. The wee man who owned the string felt sorry for the Druids and on one occasion, hid one of 'em by wrapping him up in a ball of string. The Prime Minister at the time was Balfour, and he went to Forfar to buy string in bulk. The little Scot gave Balfour a vast discount, but it wasn't until the deal was concluded that the canny Scot realized that in bringing the price down he had included the very ball of string used to hide the Druid, and that the ball of string must now have a historical value . . . Too late to retract the transaction, the Miserable Scot lamented to the Prime Minister:

'TIS A FORFAR BARTERED STRING THAT HIDE DRUID! THEN I HAVE OFFERED DOWN, BALFOUR'

John Logie Baird invented television, which was good, but from that came 'Crossroads' so the old boy has a lot to answer for.

What isn't widely known is that many years ago, the Baird clan were engaging in a feud with a band of German pirates who had landed in Scotland; nobody saw the Huns land because it was flag day in Aberdeen, and everyone was hiding.

It was a bitter struggle between them, but the Germans had superior forces and better time-keeping, and before long the Baird family were in full retreat.

Finally, only about three Baird clansmen were left in the Highlands; all the others had fled to England and social security. One night, a blood-hound tracked down the elder Baird clansman, and gripped him in its teeth as the pursuing Huns caught up with the dog. The other two members of the Baird clan tried to rescue their compatriot but to no avail, and when the Germans surrounded them, instead of being taken prisoner they decided to die by throwing themselves into a cauldron of hot borsch soup. This they did, much to the dismay of the German pirates; but as their chief said: 'No matter men, we have at least one of them in the hound's grasp, and always re-member . . .

A BAIRD IN THE HOUND IS WORTH TWO IN
THE BORSCH'

The policeman led the accused into the dock and the prisoner bowed his head as the judge thundered to him: 'Is this the first time you've been up before me?' The accused shrugged his shoulders and replied: 'I don't know . . . what time do you normally get up?' Before the judge had time to answer, the accused suddenly straightened his shoulders and shouted aloud: 'I say to you all, I do not recognize this court of my peers.' The judge said: 'Why not?' The prisoner said: 'Because you've had it redecorated.'

When the gale of laughter had subsided at this somewhat obtuse sally, the Judge sternly addressed the accused thus:

'Leonard Henry Sidebottom, you stand here accused of the crime of bigamy. All the testimony has been heard, but before I pass sentence upon you, let it be known that in this realm of ours bigamy will not be tolerated. Now the facts of the case against you. In 1967, you did marry one Kate Pickleswick in the parish of Knott-End-On-Sea. During your employment as a travelling salesman, you met and married quite unlawfully in Southend, in 1974, one Edith Tittersby. You knew at the time of the ceremony that you were committing an offence but you went through with it all the same. Let all would-be bigamists understand the gravity of such an action, and to you Leonard Henry Sidebottom, let me remind you once more that you cannot possess two women at the same time. In other words:

YOU CAN'T HAVE YOUR KATE AND EDITH'

Queen Elizabeth the First suffered from so much acid indigestion, she was prone to swell up, and when she played cards she always had the trumps.

Her handmaiden was well aware of this strange trait in the monarch, and was always careful not to dress the Queen until she'd had a right royal belch or dropped one. Then the handmaiden would chortle, 'I fart you'd do it in the end'. One day, just before the Armada came chugging up the Channel, the handmaiden had to go away to visit a sick relative, and when she got back to the Palace, she was horrified to find that someone had dressed the Queen in a hurry and already Old Bess was like a balloon . . . 'My God,' she cried. 'Look at her . . .' and thus was born a famous novel called:

GOWNED WITH THE WIND

I went to Germany once and met a miserable Hun . . . a real 'Sour Kraut'. Frankly, he talked a lot of 'Bosche', and liked his bacon without 'Rhine'. I enjoyed the German clock festival, that's where you stand still, and go: 'Tick tock'. One tourist, a man from Wales, well his wife had a face like Flint, could only say, 'Tick' and a Prussian policeman said, 'We have ways of making you tock.'

I said to one Jerry (I think he was on Pot) 'It's a long time since I was in Germany, and I've loved every minute of it . . . It's true what they say, Absence makes the heart grow fonder.' He glared at me and said: 'You misquote, my friend . . . that saying originated when it was the habit of distillers to use the spirit, absinthe to nurture a Swiss cheese dish in the Hartz mountains . . . Even today it is correct to say:

ABSINTHE MAKES THE HARTZ GROW
FONDUE'

Cleanliness in the home is quite essential if good health be the main consideration, and let's soap it will always be the case. But it can be carried to extremes. I once stayed in 'Digs' in a seaside resort, and the landlady was for ever hoovering the place up and scrubbing her gas cooker.

You simply couldn't sleep in the house for the noise of buckets and brooms, vacuums and polishers. She used to yell: 'I've hoovered one floor now I'll go in the kitchen and clean the cooker.' One of the people staying was a writer and this statement gave him the title of a book that was to become a best seller and a film as well. He called it:

ONE FLOOR HOOVERED, THE COOKER'S
NEXT

You must remember the painter Hals? He painted the famous portrait, 'The Grinning Gurkha', later changed to 'The Laughing Cavalier'. What you may not know was that as a young man he was very ready, and was known to have it away with various ladies in the West End. Hals was a noisy chap during love making, and all the women got fed up with him, until a new girl arrived who captured his heart and when he was with her he was struck dumb.

She was forbidden to tout her trade in the town, so she practised her art in an opulent tent, in fact there were three tents: one North of the Thames, one South of the river and hers, which was to the West of London. Every night Hals would be in the west tent with his desirable frump, and not a word could be heard from him. And so was born the title of a well known novel:

HALS QUIET ON THE WEST TENT FRUMP

67

Fred and Sam Surtees were friends of the great Charles Dickens. They themselves were not writers, but ornithologists, and they specialized in studying sea birds: puffins, gulls, egrets (hence the song by Edith Piaff – 'No, No Egrets'). They were not truly law abiding – they had both been up before the beak, but they were so well liked not many people would talon them. Their work took them all over and they went feather and feather away. One day they saved a sea bird called the Teal from a recently doctored cat, and they took it home with them and in time it became a pet. Charles Dickens used to play with it and when the brothers went away, and people asked him who the Teal belonged to, he would say, and the statement became the title of his new novel, 'It's

A TEAL OF TWO SURTEES'

Heard of Hughie Green? Now, Hughie Green of course hosted 'Opportunity Knocks' for many years, and did it very well too. However what isn't known to the general public is that Hughie Green was once employed as a servant in a Welsh mining town, and his employer was a writer by the name of Richard Llewelyn, that was his given name not a pen one, although he was Nibs to his neighbours because he could quill any disturbance. He looked at Hughie Green one day and got an *ink*ling about a title for his new novel, and thus was born the famous story:

HUGHIE GREEN WAS MY VALET

There is a dye works in Scotland that specializes in tinting various artifacts of heraldry: tartans, sporrans and hackles. You can have any colour you want, but the most difficult colour to attain is blue serge . . . It tends to run and is only found in the Royal College of Serge Runs. (Yes, I've used *that* one before as well.)

I had a friend who worked in the dye sheds and every time he came to our house this serge stuff would be found all over the cushions and carpets. One day the famous author, Frederick Forsyth, visited me whilst my friend from the dye works was there, and lo! Freddy got the serge dye all over his trousers. But instead of being annoyed he was delighted, because the incident gave him the title of his best selling book . . .

THE DYE OFF SERGE HACKLE

Clint Eastwood and I arc so alike . . . Butch in the face of danger and utterly fearless. If for instance, I am threatened by such awesome thugs as the wife and her mother, I resort to the old Apache Indian trick of screaming and begging for mercy. My pal Clint made a very successful movie, what they call in the business, 'A Spaghetti Western'. The film was inspired by a book whose title came from Tudor times. It appears that a nobleman, who was the ancestor of Angus Ogilvy, brought from Cairo a water gourd of great interest, and a rare volume of the great Bard, Shakespeare. It was that collection of oddities that inspired the film . . .

THE GOURD, THE BARD, AND THE OGILVY

A habit which my grandfather had always disgusted -me. He would repeatedly spit in the fireplace. Expectorating in public I find quite beyond the pale – forget the pale say I and try a bucket. (That would skuttle 'em alrighty.)

However, one day when I took my grandfather to task for doing his usual gobbing onto the hot coals, he turned to me and explained that it was through spitting that Dickens found the title of a book that he had been searching for:

GRATE EXPECTORATIONS

In Case of
Fire Please Break

THE MALADY LINGERS ON . . .

Well now . . . wasn't that an absolute hoot? As the owl said in the Bank of England, 'It's the mint with the owl'. Did you know that owls never mate in the rain, because it's too wet to woo?

So it's back to song titles again, and I'm rather glad, the others were buggers to work out. I tried to find some on carpets . . . hopeless, they were real *Carpet Buggers.*

You can have such fun with song titles, like the girl June, whose corsets snapped on the vacuum cleaner . . . and they sang:

JUNE IS BURSTING OUT ALL HOOVER

Or . . .

The religious donkey that pulled a beer cart for a living and sang:

AT THE END OF THE DRAY JUST KNEEL AND BRAY

Or . . .

The foreman in a bakery who had an employee who could slice four lots of bread at once with a meat cleaver, and the foreman would sing:

I'M LOOKING OVER A FOUR LOAF CLEAVER

The sky's the limit with them. One that can set dentures on edge is about the chap who worked at Butlin's and he hated Germans. One day a party

of Jerries came to the camp; they were pale from
working down a mine, and all they did was to sit
behind a chalet all day and drink lager. The man
from Butlin's sang to his mother that night:

'PALE HUNS I LOATHE, BEHIND THE
CHALETS MA'

I bought a house recently. I got it for 1650 . . . that was the year it was built. There's a sunken bath that goes all the way around the house – it's called a moat.

I'm not saying the walls are thin, but when the wife steam irons my vest, next door's wallpaper peels off.

The garden is in a mess, the grass is so tall every time a frog jumps up he gets a double hernia. I've had to buy a greenhouse just to grow weeds. What a cold house . . . in winter the windows steam up from the outside. I still get homesick though . . . it's my home and I am sick of it.

Here's a twist on the old song:

'FIVE FOOT TWO, EYES OF BLUE BUT OH WHAT THOSE EYES CAN DO, HAS ANYBODY SEEN MY GIRL.'

Always remember, you can kiss a nun once, or even twice but you must never get into the habit. I tried it once and developed Cloister-phobia. Well it's not *conventional* is it? What's it all abbot? I ask myself, if you've got the answer friar away.

Slumbering under a craggy bluff in North Yorkshire lies a small village called Ruff-On-The-Ole. It's so tiny the speed limit signs are back to back and tourists are given anti-blink pills. The local bank is only open on Saturdays, and that's just for hold ups.

It's a poor village, the wishing well is full of IOU's and the people take it in turn to be the village idiot. It's a hamlet of great antiquity, so old the mice are thatched, and the local store is called a 'Do It Thy Self Shop'.

I lived there a year and I got to know a nice old lady who lived in a cottage that was so remote that if you went over to borrow a cup of sugar you had to stay the night. Her only friend was shifty type called Ernie Brody, a man so crooked, he could get into a new shirt without taking the pins out.

This man wormed his way into her confidence and promised her that he would mend her only decent possession, a string of valuable pearls. Brody said he could restore the sheen to the pearls for a very nominal price. She gave them to him and that was the last anyone saw of Ernie Brody.

The poor lady sat in her old rocking chair and poured her heart out to me:

'Oh dear, my life is so wretched,' she said as she smoked a roll of bacon and inhaled deeply. 'Look at the way I live . . . The five chimney flues in this cottage are all furred up with soot, there's ice hanging in the toilet in winter, and now that they have built a pig farm on the field opposite, the view is frightful. On top of all that, the man I trusted took my pearls away to have them re-sheened and I haven't seen him since . . . Oh woe is me . . . I sit here night after night my dear sir, alone with my guitar, and I sing this plaintive song:

FIVE FURRED FLUES ICE IN'T LOO, OH WHAT A FRIGHTFUL VIEW CAN DO, HAS ERNIE BRODY SHEENED MY PEARLS?'

I was born with a banjo on my knee, it took me a week to get my trousers on. My dad was an old Indian fighter – that's what he married, an old Indian. He cleaned up such hell towns as Dodge and Houston . . . wasn't easy, he only had a small shovel. One night he rode into Tombstone, and broke his toe on it. He used to roam the prairie. I said, 'Daddy did you see a bison?' He said, 'No, we had a swill in a bucket.'

One time he was surrounded by a tribe of redskins. 'Were they Blackfeet?' I asked him. He replied, 'Don't know son, but their necks were filthy.'

On with the puns, and this time Gene Pitney's famous song comes under attack. Remember it?

'ONLY TWENTY FOUR HOURS FROM TULSA, ONLY TWENTY FOUR HOURS AWAY.'

I knew a shortsighted Indian once . . . he had a queer collection of scalps, he made hot poultices for bald indians . . . kept their wigs wam. Go on then, Sioux me . . . you don't squaw me . . . Some puns are not Apache on these.

There was a very successful Texan oil magnate . . . he was a big attraction in those parts. Everytime he dug a hole, oil came bubbling out. One well produced a thick substance that could be used for anything . . . he called it 'Amazing Grease'.

Money was no object to this man; he had two swimming pools, one always empty for those who couldn't swim, and his dog had a split level kennel. All was going well: every week a new oil tower would appear on his vast estate and he was getting fan mail from Saudi Arabia.

He sat down to dinner one night and complained to his wife that he had severe stomach pains. She said, 'Buy a new one.' He thought that remark was in bad taste, as indeed so do I, but it takes guts to tell it.

Finally he went to see a doctor who examined him most thoroughly. 'I must tell you my friend,' the doctor thundered to his patient, 'that you have ulcers and you must stop working so hard, otherwise you'll have a great deal of trouble in the future.'

The oil magnate sat there rinsing out some old money, and after he'd ironed it, he replied, 'But that's impossible. I still have to erect twenty four towers to pump out my oil, I can't stop now, the wife wants Guatemala for her birthday.' The doctor rose to his feet (he had to, he'd run out of daffodils) and said sternly, 'My friend, I am warning you if you carry on with those towers your ulcers will get worse. In other words . . .

YOU ARE ONLY TWENTY FOUR TOWERS FROM ULCERS . . . ONLY TWENTY FOUR TOWERS AWAY'

This one caused me a bit of trouble, because at the time the wife's mother was being chased by a lion. I said to the wife, 'Don't worry love, I'll rush round to the chemist.' She said, 'Why, has he got a rifle?' I said, 'No, I need a film for my camera.'

At the finish I managed to get the lion drunk and when the animal lay down in a stupor, we sat around it and had dinner . . . in other words we dined on the sotted lion.

If you think that's scraping the barrel, read on friend, as we destroy the song:

'THANK HEAVEN FOR LITTLE GIRLS, FOR LITTLE GIRLS GET BIGGER EVERY DAY'

I could have once been a human cannonball in a circus but I wasn't prepared to travel, anyway I was the wrong calibre. I always believe in keeping one's sights up, as I roam the range giving out *bullet*ins. If one sees a charabanc full of pregnant women, could it be a blunderbus? I said that once when I was on top of the Rifle Tower. (I was drunk, I'd been on the pistol four.)

The ashen-faced mourners hunched closer together as the cold grey fog embraced them in its clammy shroud. The wind howled like a lost soul in dire torment, and beyond the dark brooding rain sodden hills, a demented dwarf strangled his pet raccoon. As the coffin was lowered into its final resting place, a voice was heard to say, 'The coffin is made of elm . . . won't last, not good enough, the corpse will find his arse through it in a week.' The corpse was that of William Shakespeare, known as the Bard of Avon . . . he drank like a pike and was barred from every pub in the area. He had been a bit of a lad, he'd had his oats more often than Red Rum. He had been a prolific writer; some said the plays had been written by Bacon, but I'm convinced he used a pencil.

I went to Stratford recently and soon found myself engrossed in the history of the place, not all of it due to Bill Shakespeare. For instance, many years ago the peasants rose in revolt against certain belted Earls, and put them to death in a most peculiar manner – they roasted them on giant griddles. Legends sprang up in rural areas of the Avon, that if a well-griddled Earl's remains were seen by a beagle dog, its eyes would glaze over and lo, it could no longer be used for hunting. Many a sporting Baron went home disgusted at the sight of his beagles standing on their tails in an hypnotic state, and indeed one of them was heard to sing this plaintive song:

'THANK AVON, FOR GRIDDLED EARLS, FOR GRIDDLED EARLS GLAZE BEAGLES EVERY DAY'

81

I knew a Scotsman once who was so mean, when he found his wife in the arms of another man, he picked up his gun and shouted to his wife: 'Stand behind yer lover while I shoot you both'. What a meanie – he used to take the pendulum off the grandfather clock in case its shadow wore a hole in the wallpaper. He even had a turnstile in his purse. Ah well, it's the turn of Bonnie Scotland to have a tune garrotted . . .

'WHEN YOU WALK THROUGH THE STORM HOLD YOUR HEAD UP HIGH AND DON'T BE AFRAID OF THE DARK'

> Would you call a dwarf with asthma, semi-breve? Don't get so crotchety, it's been a tonic-sol-fah. Wait a minim, it should get better, clef-er isn't it? Besides I need the doh. Our cat plays the piano, he's an octave puss.

The other day, I was ambling along a much frequented footpath that skirts a meandering brook, and I was idly thinking about this and that – mostly that – when a small man wearing a bush hat, theatrical spats and a see-through Japanese kilt, stopped me and thrust a sheaf of documents into my hand. 'Good sir,' he cried, 'pray lend me a fiver.' I replied that I only had four pounds on me. He said, 'That's alright, you can owe me one.' The curious chap then leapt into a bush and started eating something from a bundle. I commenced to peruse the sheaf of papers, and soon became engrossed in the contents.

It appears that in the seventeenth century in Scotland, the Lairds and merchants used to protect their merchandise by using bees as a deterrent to thieves. In those far off days of yore, the quickest selling lines were skins and hides from cattle and deer, and men used to hawk these pelts throughout the highlands, only to find that swarms of angry bees would send them running for shelter.

One enterprising Scot with a face the colour of an outraged beetroot, discovered that if hawkers held the hides up in the air, and held a dirk between their teeth, the bees, all of which were drones (Are you still with me?) seemed frightened by the spectacle and so the secret of getting past the bees was finally solved, and the hawkers could carry on and solicit business at the doors of the rich. Even to this day the advice to hawkers given then, and I might add, put to a plaintive melody, can still be heard in Scotland. It goes something like this:

'WHEN YOU HAWK THROUGH A SWARM
HOLD YOUR HIDES UP HIGH . . . AND
DRONES BE AFRAID OF THE DIRK'

This is a short one but one of my favourites. I heard it from the lips of a drunk in a bar. He was sat between two men, and he turned to one and said, 'Hey pal, have you just spilt beer down my trousers?' The man shook his head and walked away. The drunk turned to the other man on his side, and repeated the question: 'Hey pal, have you spilt beer down my trousers?' The man replied that he hadn't, and the drunk said, 'Just as I suspected . . . it's an inside job'. Which takes us somewhat staggeringly into the next pun, a play on the song:

'STANDING ON THE CORNER WATCHING ALL THE GIRLS GO BY'

Crime is on the increase and the authorities seem to be powerless in the face of it, yet all the government have to do is simply nationalize it, then it will never pay for itself. My uncle Joe was a crook, a pickpocket, but he was very shortsighted and he finished up picking pockets in a nudist camp . . . yes, he was really at the bottom then. Some people will go to any lengths to avert theft. I knew a man with a bad leg called Arthur, I don't know the name of his other leg (yes, I've used *that* one before as well), but he introduced me to his sister. He said, 'Do you know my sister May?' I replied, 'No, but thanks for the tip.'

Arthur owned a bakery in Devon quite close to the sea and he found it difficult to stop seagulls swooping down and bowling his meat pies off the counter and eating them. He tried everything: he bought a dog, but everytime he shouted to it, 'Attack Rover', the dog had one. He was losing money hand over fist and as you know a baker always kneads the dough, but he used his loaf (sorry) and hired a huge gander to scare off the seagulls. Now, nearby to his bakery was a permissive sauna salon, and the gander used to perch on the roof of it and watch out for the dratted sea birds flying in to grab the meat pies. This peculiar situation inspired a hit song from the musical 'Damn Yankees'. Do you recall it?

'GANDER'S ON THE SAUNA WATCHING ALL THE GULLS BOWL PIES'

I went to see a psychiatrist last week, that's a fellow you talk to before you start talking to yourself.

He said, 'Good morning, what seems to be the trouble?' I said, 'Nobody hears a word I'm saying.' He said, 'Good morning what seems to be the trouble?' Which probably explains the nature of the next involved pun on the tune:

'HEY THERE, YOU WITH THE STARS IN YOUR EYES'

Are you getting bored? Keep on reading, that's the drill. After this it should be plane sailing. Hammer trying to amuse you, that's the tack, and vice versa.

So brace yourselves for a bit.

I enjoy travel, and with an act like mine it's a damn good thing I do. I like going by train and I always travel first class, I'm not a snob you understand, but going that way you get a better type of dust on the seats. I recently boarded a train that came from Liverpool to Euston station, and the journey only took four hours . . . mind you, I got on at Watford.

I don't mind travel by road . . . I run a Jaguar, when I bought it the salesman said, 'You'll get a lot of pleasure out of this car'. He was right – it's always a pleasure to get out of it. I'm not saying I've had a lot of trouble with it, but it even broke down on Fantasy Island. You can tell the state it's in – it's just been MOT'd by a faith healer. It badly wants four new tyres, the ones on it now are so shredded when I knock pedestrians down they get twenty lashes as they fall. It's very heavy on petrol, if you drive more than a hundred miles you become a state registered charity. Still, I always buy British, after all I'm patriotic as well as an idiot. Everywhere nowadays you see Japanese cars, and the Japs are so cocky that when you blow the horn on their new cars, it doesn't honk . . . it claps. But things are improving at British Leyland now, a shop steward was sacked recently when his union found out he'd married a commoner.

When I travel one of my favourite spots is in Portsmouth, and it was there that I heard a story that certainly chilled my blood more than an episode of 'Crossroads'.

It seems that many years ago there was a man called Aza, and he was the owner of a cooked meats shop. What people didn't know was that Aza used to murder sailors and put them in his pies. He was mad of course, because he once lost an order for a large loaf to be made in the shape of a foal. The trouble was although he actually got the thing modelled in the shape requested, he'd had a drink too many, and he lurched too wide from the oven and dropped it. He was never able to reproduce the shape. The police got wind of what he was doing and they came to the shop to arrest Aza, and they all sang:

'AZA, YOU WITH THE TARS IN YOUR PIES,
LOAVES NEVER MADE A FOAL OF YOU,
YOU ALWAYS LURCH TOO WIDE'

I'm a very unlucky person. Treets melt in my hand, and Lord Longford once mugged me. I thought of carrying around a rabbit's foot for luck, but let's face it, it didn't do the rabbit any good, I knew a man who couldn't resist backing horses; every time he made a bet, he would pluck a hair from his wife's head and wrap it around the money he was going to put on the horse. He did it for years and they are still together to this day. He's broke and she's bald.

After the silence that must have greeted that sally it's on with the word mangling, and the next song to cop it is:

'AH, SWEET MYSTERY OF LIFE AT LAST I'VE FOUND YOU . . . AND NOW I KNOW THE SECRET OF IT ALL'

Where do they prod you in the ribs and do puns? Why, the Punjab.

Some cocks actually lay eggs in India . . . they are called: Himalayas.

I once appeared in a musical based on Jewish gentlemen working in an Indian pickle factory . . . It was called, GOYS AND DILLS.

I visited the house of an Indian gentleman once, I said to his wife, 'Are you Hindu?' She said, 'We are but we're going out in a minute?'

They have food markets in Bombay called Cash and Curry's . . .

Are you sitting comfortable? Well I'll begin. Once upon a time there lived a fleet-footed Scotsman called Master Ray and he hailed from the town of Leith. He was a man who was violently opposed to the British forces who were occupying Scotland, and he used to creep down from the highlands, hit soldiers on the head with his club, then run away like greased lightning to his small boat, which was named: 'De Ghoul'. The tiny craft was moored in a Loch near to Leith and it proved to be an excellent means of escape for the wily rascal. However it couldn't last, and one day an enterprising young cavalry officer hid behind a rock and waited for the arrival of swift Master Ray. His patience was rewarded and as the Scot crept towards the camp, the officer leapt out, clasped the bandit tightly to his tunic and before the bemused Scot could get away, the officer had bound him with chains. Meanwhile, one of the officer's men came to report that rats had gnawed the main rings of the 'De Ghoul' and the ropes mooring the boat had come adrift from the rings holding it secure. As the famous Master Ray was being taken into custody, the regiment all stood to attention as the officer who had captured him sang:

'AH, SWIFT MASTER RAY OF LEITH I'VE CLASPED AND BOUND YOU ... AND NOW THE RATS HAVE GNAWED THE MAIN RINGS OF DE GHOUL'

A chap called to my house one night, he had a row of medals on his chest. I said to him: 'I see you've been at the front?' He said, 'Yes, I couldn't get any answer so I came round the back.' He said proudly, 'I'm Irish.' I said, 'Oh really?' He said, 'No, O'Toole.' Suddenly he produced a gun and snarled, 'Stick 'em up.' I said, 'Stick what up?' He shook his head and said, 'I'm not sure, I'm new at the game.' What a gangster he was, his gang actually broke into Fort Knox and picked the lead off the roof.

Okay, you've had enough, well here's a cute pun for you to savour. I've based it on the old song:

'GALWAY BAY'

I once worked in a soap factory but it was only to tide me over.
I couldn't have stood it for long, not on your life boy.
I wore jeans and a lather belt, and struck a bold figure.
The job didn't *dazz*le me, most of the men I worked with thought I was a surf.
I made a packet out of it, but went ill and flaked out. (What a silly sud I was.)

This one is a pure stinker I warn you, and should only be told if one is conversant with the subject proper, or well and truly stoned out of one's mind . . . Here goes nothing!

Many years ago, an Irish farmer called Paddy Hugh made quite a living by shipping his prize heifers over to Thailand. Firstly he shipped them to Chester, where they were put in boats on the river Dee to get used to the long sea journey, and then on to Bangkok. The cows hated being made to cruise down the river, their milk curdled and they couldn't have a smoke. Naturally the beasts revolted in the oddest fashion. Once they got to Thailand, they deliberately gnawed the feet of a very expensive Indian fakir, a holy man or seer as we would say. Hugh's farm hands were sick of the whole business and would prefer to keep out of the way and sit for hours washing away the dirt from rice plants that grew at the base of the Mountains of Mourne (very rare rice this, makes an excellent curried shamrock). Although it was a tedious job they could at least watch Mrs Gladys O'Mara building her dyke across a small brook, to use as irrigation. Gladys's son was a scientist and one of his chief interests was to cross ducks with horses; apart from helping ducks to be free of frustration, it was a classic case of macabre breeding. The horses belonged to the flute player, James Galway, the ducks to Gladys. Soon people from far and wide would sit and rinse the Mourne rice and enjoy the spectacle of horse and duck mating.

Hugh was left to look after his heifers and the Dee travel not to mention the fact that the cows were still gnawing the seer's feet and this particular occurrence prompted the birth of a well known song that you can still hear to this day:

'IF HUGH'S HEIFERS GNAW A COSTLY SEER
    TO THAILAND,
IF ONLY HATING CRUISING OFF THE DEE.
YOU CAN SIT AND WASH THE MOURNE RICE
    OVER GLAD'S DYKE,
AND SEE THE SON GROW DOWN ON
    GALWAY'S BAY'

When I was washed up on a desert island, a young nubile girl found me and tended to my injuries. I began to recover but she could see that I was unhappy, and asked me what I wanted most as she leant, naked, over me. I said I missed good old fashioned beer, so she made me a tub of it. Still sensing that I was sad, she again asked me what I wanted. I replied, 'cigarettes' and lo and behold, the dusky beauty rolled me several first class cigarettes. Then she kissed me and whispered throatily, 'Now we go inside my hut and play a game.' I looked at her with love and said, 'Don't tell me you've got a dartboard as well?'

On the theme of desert islands, yet another frisky pun, on the song:

'THE SONG HAS ENDED BUT THE MELODY LINGERS ON'

Chinese priests used to use women captives as targets for their spears, hence the song, 'Buddha can you spear a dame?' My cat is Chinese, he's a Peking tom. Where do you buy a boat from in China? Junk shops.

When a Chinaman has toothache the time is always the same: Tooth thirty . . . they know a lot about pork, they are full of pig tales.

Slightly to the left of the island of Bali, is a tiny palm fringed atoll that is the home of a gentle people called the Mukk. Their leader is a fine man known to all as M'uni. He goes everywhere with his kinsfolk, in fact they have a saying in the East which, translated, reads, 'Where there's Mukk there's M'uni'.

The atoll is noted for the good health of the inhabitants, and they put it down to the magical powers of a sacred sarong which is hung on the wall of a temple.

When anybody feels ill, they simply enter the temple, roll themselves in the sarong, and lo! within a few minutes, they are cured and are ready to go back on the beach to smoke fish. Obviously over the years the sarong had got a bit filthy, because the natives aren't very hygenically minded . . . in most of their houses, the safest place to keep money is under the soap.

At any rate, M'uni decided to have the sarong washed and dried in a huge copper urn. After this had been accomplished, it was put back in the temple and the first person to use it again was an elderly native with gout and tennis elbow. He rolled himself up in the sarong and waited . . . Dear reader, this time there was no cure forthcoming, the sarong had failed. Sadness and fear pervaded the atoll, and VAT was introduced.

One day a cyclonic wind blew a schooner onto the rocks, and the only survivors, were the captain, one Hugh Tremain, and a French nobleman, a knight from Argonne. They soon heard of the atoll's problem and they agreed to help by buying a plot of land on which they built a clinic in which to produce a linctus to fight the contagious maladies that might afflict the natives. They called it 'The Malady Zone'.

M'uni decided to get his people together and tell them all about it, and even to this day, a song still can be heard in the islands of the Pacific:

'THE SARONG IS URN DRIED, BUT THE MALADY LINGERS ON. HUGH AND THE KNIGHT ARGONNE, BOUGHT THE MALADY LINCTUS ZONE'

It should have been the mother-in-law's funeral tomorrow, but she's cancelled it. Now there's a woman for you ... I think. She calls me effeminate, and next to her I am. She never stops talking, her mouth is open so often in winter we lag her tonsils. She's so fat that when she crosses her legs it looks like two sides of gammon in a stranglehold. This pun is dedicated to her, and I hope it chokes her ... The song?

'BLUES IN THE NIGHT
(MY POPPA DON' TOLD ME WHEN I WAS IN
KNEE PANTS ...)'

I play golf; but not well – I have a fair way to go yet. I enjoy the game but always stop for tea. I'm never hungry on the course, I have a sand wedge. Actually, I'm a divotee of the game, and always play with something on my head like a handy cap.

Golf courses are haunted ... they are full of bogies ... It's true, ask my par.

A strange tale indeed! A pretty kettle of fish! A fine panikin of turbot! Oh yes, I'm a dab hand at fish, I never flounder at all, after all there is no business like shoal business.

Many years ago when I was a mere stripling, a family heirloom came into my possession ... a pair of Marshal Ney's underpants. Who is Marshal Ney, you may ask? Marshal Ney, my uneducated friend, was Napoleon's best soldier, who got old Boney's troops back from Moscow; but in doing so his drawers froze solid and for years, after my great-great-great-grandfather pinched them, our family used them to wash in. They were wider than a basin and more reliable.

Near where we lived was an old Indian lady called May, who used a giant popadum as an oracle, not as something to eat with vindaloo.

Well, one day a weary-looking, worn-out nun came trudging past our house, and told me she was God. I suspected she was half mad, but nuns have always scared me, and I can't get out of the habit . . . (sorry).

She ranted on and on, and I vainly looked around for someone to rescue me from the poor good lady. Suddenly the giant popadum spoke to the nun and commanded the lady to go, saying, 'I am the oracle, and I say you are not God . . . you are not Divine'. I stared open-mouthed as I absently began to wash myself down in Ney's underpants. The nun threw a clump of groundsel at the popadum, but it ignored it, and I sang this song which I have never forgotten.

'MAY'S POPADUM TOLD ME WHEN I WASHED
IN NEY'S PANTS . . . A WORN NUN IS
NOT GOD, SON'

I feel sorry for race horses, their lives are full of Epsom Downs . . . (a fetlock of good that pun did). Some, of course, horses I mean naturally, have a more stable disposition, unlike others who don't know their oats and clutch at straws. But in the mane, nags are nice creatures; some don't like water, and it was a bad day when the 'Reins' came down. Saddlely, some horses are classed as old hacks and their drays are numbered.

What this has to do with the next play on words saga I'll never know, but here we venture forth to bungle the song:

'SHOULD OLD ACQUAINTANCE BE FORGOT, AND NEVER BROUGHT TO MIND' ETC.

I did have a pun about a castle, but it will *keep* for now, anyway it was only really an after*Fort*. (My wife said she'd like to *Schloss* me for that.) I think we should make the *Moat* of castles, after all the *Knights* are drawing in, and *Joust* you wait 'til winter *combs*.

We must never forget the early pioneers of the cinema industry. Those intrepid men and women who brought celluloid illusion onto the screens, to bring a little colour into our drab lives. One such man was Arthur Quince, the very first film stuntman.

For years he worked for a rather unlucky studio: Pennine Pictures Ltd, Milnrow. They never seemed to get it right; for instance, in 1921, the studio produced films like 'All Quiet On the Eastern Front', 'For Whom The Bell Whistles', 'The Three Feathers' and 'Gone With The Breeze'. But, despite the fact most of Pennine Pictures were a box office flop, Arthur Quince was very popular indeed. Utterly fearless, he had been blown up, shot at, poisoned and hung from an elm; then his wife left him. He died at the ripe old age of twenty-three whilst playing the part of Nero in the spectacle 'George Hur'. It was a dreadful demise. As Quince fiddled while Rome burnt, he was eaten by a deaf lion and with his death, Pennine Pictures went broke, and the studio is now a warehouse for tractor tyres and rivets.

In Rochdale, where Arthur Quince was most adored, they put plaques up at every street corner to commemorate Quince and his stunts, and for years his admirers could gather and recall his great moments. Then in 1965 a tall, well-dressed Sikh came to Rochdale with a promise to bring prosperity to the town with his business, which was the manufacturing of gold signs for hanging outside pubs and offices and so on . . . Soon, vans carrying the name 'Gold-Hang-Signs' were everywhere. As things at the time were fairly rough, the townsfolk welcomed the eastern gentleman until he loftily informed them that all the Arthur Quince plaques must come down to make way for his gold hanging signs. Fury exploded and the community was split by the bombshell. Finally, in the Town Hall, the issue came to a head. One man alone summed up the feelings of many when he stood before the council and gave his impassioned oratory. His name was Sam Bloggs, and he thundered forth, 'Will Gold-Hang Signs give us the pleasure Arthur Quince did? I ask you to raise enough money for us to save the plaques so that Arthur will never be erased from our thoughts . . . In other words:

'SHOULD ALL ARTHUR QUINCE STUNTS BE
    FORGOT
AND NEVER BOUGHT TO REMIND.
SHOULD ALL ARTHUR QUINCE STUNTS BE
    FORGOT
FOR THE SIKH OF GOLD HANG SIGNS'

As a writer, I find Spain a fascinating country. I adore the people and they certainly know their onions. The language is colourful, is it not? They even call their navy the 'Senor Service'.

Perhaps the most controversial aspect of Spanish life and custom, is the Corrida Del Toro ... the bullfight. The drama of death in the arena of sand: the heat, the smell of outraged animals, the hot sun beating down onto the heads of the engrossed throng ... The magnificence of the matador, the picador, the front door, ah!

It was some two years ago when I was in Espana. I was there to learn the language of Iberia, a tongue that is fruitful and heady. I recall that I was studying the verb 'To Have' which in Spanish is 'Tengo'. A flamenco dancer was my teacher and we often danced together, and why not? After all, it takes two to tengo. (My apologies to all package tour operators.)

One night I met a Spanish comedian, not a big name in the world of show business, in fact he was a club 'turn'. Nice man, his name was Enrico Diaz, and he and his six brothers had just attended a funeral wake; not surprising, because as you know there are seven diaz in a wake. His burning ambition was to become a bullfighter like his father, now retired of course but still shipping bulls for the contests. (Actually, Senor Diaz was the biggest bull shipper in Barcelona.)

Enrico took me to my first bullfight and he was on the edge of his seat with excitement. Suddenly, to my horror, he could contain himself no longer, and as the mighty bull cantered into the ring, Enrico leapt into the arena and charged the bull, waving his waistcoat as he did. It was over in seconds. The maddened bull struck Enrico in the small of his back and as he lay in agony upon the blood-drenched sand, the bull gored the little club turn to death.

There was a shocked silence, and with tears streaming down his coarsened features, Enrico's father put his hand on my shoulder and said sadly, 'You, my friend, are a writer, and you must write a book about my son's death.' I did and I called the book:

'ONE GORED TURN DESERVES AN AUTHOR'

On the following pages are details of Arrow books that will be of interest.

A LITTLE ZIT ON THE SIDE

Jasper Carrott

He's been a delivery boy (the terror of Solihull), a toothpaste salesman (for four hours), a folkie (repertoire – two songs) – and the most unlikely and original comic superstar for years.

Now Jasper Carrott reveals more of the outrageous talent that has taken him from the Boggery to a series of one-man shows that won him ITV's Personality of the Year Award.

Discover the do-it-yourself man, how to become star of Top of the Pops and the Carrott guide to dog-training. Relive the simple pleasures of The Magic Roundabout, Funky Moped and the Mole.

£1.25

THE UNLUCKIEST MAN IN THE WORLD
and similar disasters

Mike Harding

Born in the picturesque spa of Lower Crumpsall, he spent his early years in the brooding shadow of a cream cracker factory. At the age of seventeen he bought a set of Mongolian bagpipes and joined a rock and roll band. Much of his manhood has been spent waiting for a girl wearing red feathers and a hulu skirt to come into his life. He is the incorrigible, irrepressible and slightly mad Mike Harding.

The Unluckiest Man in the World takes us into the world of Mike Harding with an inimitable collection of happy, sad, ridiculous, profound and simply hilarious songs, poems and stories.

£1.25

A. J. WENTWORTH, BA

H. F. Ellis

'One of the funniest books ever . . . it deserves to follow *The Henry Root Letters* to the top of the bestsellers' *Sunday Express*

There is chalk in his fingernails and paper darts fill the air as A. J. Wentworth, BA, mathematics master at Burgrove Preparatory School, unwittingly opens the doors that lead not to knowledge but to chaos and confusion. Here are his collected papers in which you can at last discover the truth about the fishing incident in the boot room, the real story about the theft of the headmaster's potted plant, and even the answer to the sensitive question of whether or not Mr Wentworth was trying to have carnal knowledge of matron on that one, memorable occasion.

'I did indeed laugh aloud till I cried' *Graham Lord, Sunday Express*

'A book of such hilarious nature that I had to give up reading it in public as my shrieks were causing both surprise and annoyance to those present' *Arthur Marshall, New Statesman*

'Few books have made me laugh out loud quite so often' *Christopher Matthew, Evening Standard*

£1.25

BESTSELLING NON-FICTION FROM ARROW

All these books are available from your bookshop or news-agent or you can order them direct. Just tick the titles you want and complete the form below.

☐	THE GREAT ESCAPE	Paul Brickhill	£1.60
☐	A RUMOUR OF WAR	Philip Caputo	£1.95
☐	SS WEREWOLF	Charles Whiting	£1.50
☐	A LITTLE ZIT ON THE SIDE	Jasper Carrott	£1.25
☐	ART OF COARSE ACTING	Michael Green	£1.25
☐	UNLUCKIEST MAN IN THE WORLD	Mike Harding	£1.25
☐	DIARY OF A SOMEBODY	Christopher Matthew	£1.25
☐	TALES FROM A LONG ROOM	Peter Tinniswood	£1.50
☐	LOVE WITHOUT FEAR	Eustace Chesser	£1.50
☐	NO CHANGE	Wendy Cooper	75p
☐	MEN IN LOVE	Nancy Friday	£1.95

Postage _____

Total _____

ARROW BOOKS, BOOKSERVICE BY POST, PO BOX 29, DOUGLAS, ISLE OF MAN, BRITISH ISLES

Please enclose a cheque or postal order made out to Arrow Books Limited for the amount due including 10p per book for postage and packing for orders within the UK and 12p for overseas orders.

Please print clearly

NAME ....

ADDRESS ....

....

Whilst every effort is made to keep prices down and to keep popular books in print, Arrow Books cannot guarantee that prices will be the same as those advertised here or that the books will be available.